Springtime In Moldova

Springtime In Moldova

Poems by

Hanoch Guy-Kaner

Cover Shay Culligan

ISBN: 978-1-950462-02-5

Kelsay Books Inc.

kelsaybooks.com

502 S 1040 E, A119
American Fork,Utah 84003

Although the dream is a very strange phenomenon and an inexplicable mystery, far more inexplicable is the mystery and aspect our minds confer on certain objects and aspects of life.
–Giorgio de Chirico

We are such stuff as dreams are made on
–William Shakespeare, *The Tempest*

Acknowledgments

Turtle Ink Press: "Pardon," 2010.

Apiary: "Eine kliene nacht music," Winter/Spring 2011.

Apiary: "Silkworms," Winter 2013.

Musehouse Journal: "Nothing peculiar," Spring 2013.

Ink: "Mamamaldragon," 2014.

Amulet: "Beyond Magritte," "Claimed," January 2015.

In Between Hangovers: "When," first published as "Spell,"
    August 2016.

In Between Hangovers: "Boots," "Brushes," October 2016.

Contents

Pardon

Predawn masks the window.

I miss the last first train.
An old woman takes off her dress.
Reveals: a diaper.
A homeless man with new Nike sneakers
waltzes me around the benches.
I throw him onto the tracks.

I am dragged to the courthouse.
The woman testifies.
The buxom judge nurses
the bald guard.
I stare.
I confess.
I pardon myself,
dance on the roof.
I clutch my heart,
catching a grenade,
rolling on a bridge.

Springtime in Moldova

A.

I enter a room with a thin pencil.
A naked man shows perfect teeth.
His foreskin shines.
He is mending a purple sock.
I write my confession on his back.
Ink stains turn into swirls.
The naked man whines and twists.
By the way, you can choose your burial date.

B.

Springtime in Moldova.
Dandelions have the nerve
to cover the war cemetery.
Tombstones trying on different skirts
brought in by a fat seamstress
who chases me around the cemetery
demanding I put her back in my will.

C

The thin man pees on the ceiling.
I have to fill my fountain pen.
My confession multiplies,
published in evening papers.

D

Fleas climb the court doorman tattered fur coat.
He stamps my confession: *Return to sender unknown.*
Interrogators are buried under paper stacks.
The thin man on the ceiling shouts a court date in 2010.
Take off your clothes. You can borrow my socks.

E.

Still springtime in Moldova.
Battles rage on in the mountains
between rebels and royalists.
The naked man sharpens a thin pencil,
sticks it behind his ear, sends me
on a mission to find figs.

F.

The war moves down to the valley by the sea.
Enemies take a break, play soccer in the mud.
My blank confession marked *illegible language*
lands in the thin man's open casket.

(*Inspired by Bob Dylan*)

13

Concrete

I run to 94th street

through square cloned houses

sharp with gravel.

The bridge greenlights me.

A rusty boat stuck at the jetty

with a penguin.

I am kind to the heatherbeach

A peeling gilded angel sticks

a "Heil Hitler" cross in my chest.

Am I guilty?

Crows confirm.

I am fed my morning yogurt.

A flag pole collapses on top of me.

A wheelbarrow drags me

mixed with concrete of a new house.

Marienbad

Snow wrapped the statues in Marienbad's fountains by the gate
It was summer in Carlsbad we swam with swans in the pond
J'aime Brahms you said
but refused to dance in the castle's great hall
I am haunted by the green strapless gown
you will wear at the ball
The golden cross is an omen we will meet next year
Last year I gave you an amber bracelet by the beach

We never met again after we were married
by Hans the priest on Venice beach
You are exquisitely beautiful on the balcony
overlooking the palace's garden
Another man kissed me on the neck
in the hot spring last year
Three years since my husband made love
among fireflies to a blonde in the pond

It is too late to rekindle our lust
after the queen's ball
We took a mud bath while the lion guards
slept by the castle

I will bleed on the shinning marble next year
Last year you were found floating in the pond
They are unable to find our bodies by hell's gate

Mammaldragons

Reptiles leave
clumsy footprints
In our nights
Our mammal short life
is littered with lizards
who strike with fierce tails
Our friends recoil
retreat as enemies pursue
into our burrow
We are startled
by mice memories

Too weak
to defend our territory
we weep
When fire rages
despair drives us
to the ocean
to join the fishes
We cling to them
They shake us off
till we drown
or come to our senses
in the last second

Silkworms

In 1950 the yellow red striped hairy silkworms
I collected all day off the mulberry tree
scattered all over the eastern porch.
My aunt shoots me a sick glare.

Dying lime tree sighs.
Golden quinces have haloes.
Hunger unhinges the door to
my Mother's compote.

Another son of the milkman killed in action.
Seventeen-year old David
died hitting a mine.
His father Shimon the milkman started humming.
Above my head hordes of killer bees.

Only a sliver of light on the porch.
I forget to feed the silkworms mulberries.
        They jump off the porch.

My two bullies Dan and Uri
keep hitting me hard.
In the olive grove.
An old Arab chases them
with a crooked stick.

In 1955 we dig trenches
To hide from Iraqi warplanes
Our wooden guns smell of grease.

On the northern porch, I sit on
the broken step.
Birds shatter with a sick heart
for Ruthie who moved to Iran.

Our patrol car hits a pot hole
on the dirt road where
a huge tractor wheels
are twisted by a mine.
An ostrich runs across
the road tom the border.

Quinces shed their plumes on the eastern porch.
The lime tree corpse on the ground.
        By it a dead hairy silkworm in a tin tub.

        I don't believe in light.

Eine kliene nacht musik

Stars are sharp.

I step on a hissing meteor.

Clumsy I tear a morning cloud

Commanded to sweep the earth with a feather.

In the Sahara desert, vipers befriend me.

Compelled, I comply.

Neptune sticks a seaweed pitchfork

In my eye,

Halves a mermaid.

I swim the covered planet

To a no-island

Climb a non-mountain

Kicked back to solid

Sky.

Claimed

They come out of the thick fog.

I am knocked out

by their foul sulfur breath.

Their straw beards

claw my chest, they

demand what's theirs.

I run in the muddy darkness

along electrified barbed wire fence,

join the long lines of shadows.

Denied a bowl of soup.

Thrown into a moving truck.

Dumped into a ditch.

In the middle of raging war games,

shells explode.

Wrapped in a camouflage tank net,

I shiver in the cold desert.

A black scorpion stings.

My chest blows up.

I am claimed by ghosts

in a swirling sand storm.

Nothing peculiar

about the small boy.

Awake on an army cot,

in a shack at the end of a

houseless treeless street.

Aunts left.

Sleepers worn out.

Cap lost.

He grabs a grapefruit through the window.

Tears its flesh, scrapes the rind,

downs two cups of glistening sugar.

Smashes the honey jar to get to the bottom.

Barefoot he takes cautious steps

about the shack, counts them twice.

Backs away from an aged face in the mirror.

He drinks out of the hose,

unwashed grapes

stain his undershirt.

Oil lamp shadows

on the scratched walls.

A head tears the screen,

a hiss by his face.

No additions

A place with no additions.
No dos or don'ts, or musts or shoulds or else.
Just buts and maybes and divided zeroes.
Where one and two make twenty-one,
Where circles within circles tremble.
Rectangles tango with master triangles.
Rectangles tango with the squares,
Where circles within circles tremble,
Where one and two make twenty-one.

Just buts and maybes and divided zeroes.
No do's or don'ts or musts or shoulds or else.
It is a place with no additions.

Crabapple

Border bookstore at the top of the hill is dark.

Graffiti swastikas on the doors.

The Hungry Heart
padlocked due to an eviction.
Trash blocks the windows.

Red clay road dotted
with yellow acacia balls by the olive grove
collapsed on top of a shot paratrooper.

Crushed houses spit dust covered children
chased by wild dogs to a mine field.
Low flying jets, torn roads,
terrified refugees into ditches.

Dan thin as a rail was mugged by cancer.
His obese neighbor Scott strangled by a heart attack
at the corner of his parents' hot tub.
Crabapple and a maple tree struck by lightning,
wires set on fire, total my Honda.

Mordecai's last second left him with a gaping mouth,
his chin digging his chest
on January 5th 2010.

Mailman's innocence

On Harrison Avenue
chainsaw chops down Gingko trees
spreading yellow stinky fruits.

The mower fires up short bursts,
barks at the tall grass.

The creek changes course
from the Delaware to the mountains
confusing squirrels
and geese.

Aram fires a pistol,
cheers on white poodles
sporting striped sweaters.

The mailman
proclaims innocence
as to Greece's
financial collapse.

An ordinary night in Elkins Park

The house on Mill's corner stretches,
its walls yawn,
slides on mud to the creek.
The basement trades places with the attic.
Kids' beds hang upside down.
They travel to Israel in their sleep.
The wind puts a French sign
on 259 rue Ashbourne door.
Hydrangea in the front switches
with the azalea in the back.
The deck is stuck to the side wall.
Burglars get confused and surrender.

At this moment

Hundreds of thousands of bodies wash to shore
A volcanic eruption at sea submerges twenty islands
forest fires leave piles of charred redwood trees
a glacier sails away carrying a family of polar bears
Layers of stars get entangled in strings
shaking them off into a network of milky ways
The St. John river flows away from the bay of Fundy
Cars go backwards on Magnetic Hill

The creek in my back yard is
as huge as the Nile or the Amazon
and is still polishing pebbles,
Mallards fly over
The birch tree splits dies and
falls into the water

The torn balloon was once the sky dome
Yellow and red balls left by little Lilly
contain the code for future universes

Evening touches morning
Night swallows high noon

"At this moment I realized that I did not know anything for certain."*
* Tadeusz Borowski
1922-1951

Our eyes register the light of dead stars*

Our eyes register the light of dead stars.
One of them dubbed NT 2248
was our warm home
where pale grasses soared to red rooftops
where purple columbines blossomed on our window sills.
Where we nestled our dreams.

The planet was the origin of
the great exodus 521,000,000 years ago.
We were not warned that we violated
one of the seven hundred-twenty-three injunctions.
Kicked out by the whim of a disgruntled locksmith named Job.

We traveled with turtle houses on our backs
across the expanses of shadow holes,
crossed moon galaxies,
cut by star shards,
shoved into snowy sky caves,
charred by comet tails.

Torn skinned dumped on
a planet of tin hot roofs,
strapped to metal chairs,
we emit monosyllabic groans
and fall silent.

*André Schwarz-Bart, *The Last of the Just*

Memories

Asphalt weeping into sidewalks
Crushing ice splits them apart.
In the Kmart parking lot
homeless men drag around
blankets on leashes.

Coffee cups spill over bank customers
going through revolving doors.
Mall crowd looks up in unison
at a pair of parrots screaming:
No sales today

The carousel comes to a screeching halt
throwing off parents and children.
A giant hand yanks off horses' heads
onto a truck speeding to an antique road show.

Wheelbarrows dump patients
with IV's in their arms
on San Francisco sidewalks.
A small boy in red trunks is snatched by his kite.
A dad, helpless, on golden sand.

We are stunned by the final notice.
Grace period expired.
Woods retreat across the Mexican border
Hiding cartel corpses.

Chirping crickets

The kitchen floor is spotless
The refrigerator dishwasher humming
Stains disappear from the ceiling

The yard stays under twilight spell
Trees stuck between seasons coated with light snow
leaves half shiny half brown under warm rain

The highway by the house shrinks to a donkey path
Weeds retreat underground with a whimper
Woodchucks move their families across the street

Not one squirrel to be seen
Cardinals blue jays and finch pairs missing
Earthworms hang dry on crumbling a stone wall

Synagogue mournful Yom Kippur shofar
mixes with the Romanian church requiem
cut by fire sirens

Rooms full of chirping crickets
From the low hills hyenas and jackals descend

Skycurrents

(for Karen)

Leave the bed unmade,
Leap to the ceiling with your cat.
Walk on your hands.

Open the windows.
Let the wind scatter bills articles and
unedited magazines.

Grow wings on the roof.
Land on Bonnard's pink porch.
Parachute to Dakota's badlands,
greet Teddy Roosevelt.

Ride an elephant
through Kipling's jungle.
Fly with Antoine and dance
with the Little Prince.

Beyond Magritte

I fashion huge clay pots in my kiln
Fire my hot air balloon at 3am
Fall exhausted into a coffin

I proudly wear my black beret
Have a pallet of vibrant colors
My finger draws a figure in a coffin

Sky scraps in the closet
Chain the sun to the dog's house

Squash the moon into a coffin

I bow in the Umayyad mosque in Cordoba
Marvel at the Quran blue calligraphy
Muhammad rises from his coffin

Bonnard hosts me on a fragrant pink porch
I float on Monet's lily pond
Picasso paints his coffin

A groundhog runs over a dung beetle
Wasps pay their respects,
roll it in a grass coffin

I shop for a bargain crate at Wall mart,
change my mind, get cremated

Empty grave and coffin

Flowers

Crumbling lines
inside the veins
a small bowing black boy
flogged by a giant
hammered by heart beats,
falling forward and backward
growing paler and paler

Sliding trees in a storm
fading lines into darkness
vanishing darkness
collapsing spaces into themselves
little infinities in agony
dying children in a plague

Mountscapes

A green cow

   in a white meadow

Silver strips
          rustle

Razor beams
cut
poppies

Valley
climbs
  to mount
  in folds

        Huffing
             Puffing

Hill terrace
     light
a green cow
in a white meadow

On the healing day

Lucky coins roll down the hill.
Chimney sweepers flirt with
beautiful street captains,
party with chimps.
Imprisoned fairies push out window bars,
lick honey jars.

A stern Lolita chides snow white
for being sucked into the myth,
while Alice breaks mirrors,
cries out for Peter Pan.

In the town square below the twisted clock,
Istavan and Melchior dance a fancy polka
in purple mini-skirts.
Avram chases a blue smoke rings
down the cobbled alleys.

In the sky, tiny angels
ride giraffes
with streaking comets.

Busy Friday

Whale moon belly opens wide.
Time for Friday giant flea market
where you can find anything your heart desires:
bargain newborn stars
small meteors
slightly used shuttles
armor against invaders
fragrant vanilla dipped rocks
smooth blue touch tofu.

Enjoy watching purple cows grazing
Licking noisy Popsicles
Giraffes play sugarball catch
Oops, they dropped one on

Mrs. Goldie Schwarz
in her kitchen in Philadelphia
already has a headache
trying to cook gefilte fish for the holiday.

Her husband Dr. Professor Mortimer Schwartz M.D., Ph.D.
calls to say that he is going to cook tonight,
because he will bring to dinner two llamas.
"Did I say llamas? I meant penguins."

Mrs. Schwartz faints.
Her mother threatens suicide.
Meanwhile the fish have had it.
They take off to the moon
where the cook promptly grills them
and serves them to black holes.
Black holes have to eat too.

A polite pig offers:

"s'il vous plait fromage paunte?"
The moon declines: "Non, merci."
The pig throws the cheese into space saying:
"Catch, Yo dude," and a dragon gobbles it up.

Meanwhile Mrs. Schwartz
and her mother are revived,
not astounded to see through the glass wall
elderly men beating each other
with bushes in the bathhouse
then flying above the city.

The moon wipes her sweaty forehead,
orders angel brooms to clean up the place.

Thursday noon

When I was born, I was two years old
My parents thought that it was pretty odd

I winked and blinked and dressed myself
Aunts and uncles thought me an elf

But by then I was already twelve
The magic and the wonder gone

I felt like a blind mole in a hole,
very puzzled, perturbed and restless

But had a feeling my destiny was greatness
I did not grow except my toes and shoes
till I chanced upon a busy bee hive that buzzed the news

that I was I conceived on Hydra a Pluto moon
and they would come for me on Thursday noon

You should listen well for bells of a balloon
Indeed, a colorful balloon landed Thursday noon
It barely missed the pool and auntie Kroon

The pilot dressed as a giant clown sprayed me with a hose
I was stunned to see my ears grow to a meter .so did my nose

On planet Hydra moon you do not want to be an oddball

Where we compete whose ears are huge and play nose ball
eat tree bark fly upside down and that's not all

We took off in hurry with rainbow smoke
and the pilot clown told me stories that made the time pass

You will love our purple skies, our ruby seas and long days that last
We wear ice cream fedora hats
that cool us down then we eat them fast

Our school days last about an hour in the moon and sun,
the school year ends after a month with silliness and fun

For work we play, we dance, we jump into the hay
We get rewarded by flights in space throughout the Milky Way

and tell bizarre tales of stupid earthlings' wars, waste
presidents, congressmen and mayors lack of taste

As for us every body votes all the animals and trees
even snakes, lizards, raccoons, hippos, elephants and bees

Nobody ever knows the outcome of the voting
but the elections always end with the biggest outing

If you aren't careful you'll fall into goulash pit meat
Hungarian paprika will be poured on you to eat.

A gourmet sandwich, which took you an hour to prepare
Will be snatched from you by a tiny bear

you'll be offered a little camel for your trouble
If you complain you'll get a llama double.

All in the spirit of fun, summersaults and games
Lightness, frivolity and belly laughs are our aims

On Sunday mornings, we are obliged to tell joke or mime
followed by a play, a long fairytale, if there is time

There is no censorship on what we imagine, think or dream
Mondays each family spends in a hot tub and relaxes as a team

On Tuesdays, all streets are closed and giant newsprints spread
to paint and draw cartoons write poems, songs and tales of dread.

Wednesdays are days of rest
Thursdays spent in craziness and jest

We don't have cars, oil or coal nothing of those ills
We get our power from the stars and moon mills

At birth, each one of us is issued a red bike with wings
And we exchange it as we grow and feel like kings

What earthlings do in years and pay a lot of taxes
We do in minutes, seconds or just give them the axes

So there's a chime ringing two or three or four or five
And that's how old the newborn is and they really thrive

If you'd like to visit wait by the beehive on a Thursday noon
and you'll certainly be picked up by a colorful balloon

Lightseeds

(for Salvador Dali and Pieta)

One moves
uncomfortably
beckoned by
mysterious sky signals.

All seeds stir.
One by one they shoot out seeking
hidden dark discs in the skies,
tracking them, chasing them,
tricking them into submission.

Penetrating them, the seeds linger inside
until the discs stretch, enlarge,
in a joyful flight into orbit,
become light spheres,
colliding playfully with each other.

They cross heavy curtains of abandoned stars,
disappear behind them,
ringing their bells through veils,
looking into vast extinguished spaces.

Overcome by a searing longing
for their luminous sunflower mother
they tear the walls of the lightspheres,
leaving them bleeding.

Falling fast, dry seeds scatter
between star junk piles blown
by storms into fierce galaxies and
extinguished mountainous planets.

Frozen lightless seeds shells ripped open,
swallowed by hissing flames,
except one who
continues the impossible
journey back.

I do not predict rain

Cats and owners crawling
in barbed wire chicken coops.
Tall masked guards pointing rifles.

Huge rusty ponds extend
throughout the land
where small albino fish
lie listlessly at the bottom
surrounded by sparkling salt rocks.

Windmills duel with
oil rigs in Texas
Struck by lightning
fall like giant upside down roaches.
Corn stalks laugh hysterically.

A bridge splits in four
falls into the Mississippi
with a school bus.
Victims trapped in twisted metal
deposited by currents in a dam.
Salmon watch.

Spiked black lava
takes over east west roads.
Children jump rope
till they lose their minds.

Last call

Let the leopard
hang the antelope
The mongoose
terrorizes the chickens.
The weeds trap wheelbarrows.
Dense leaves choke the roof.
Water skips on the broken steps.

Let drought rule,
Crack the earth.
Sharp roots
violate crumbling houses.
Mudslides rush from the hills.
Let mold streak the city walls
sickening the enemy.

Roaring water falls
into icy ponds
guarding stillness
at the end of the day
punctuated by owl's calls.

Mosquito infested pools
fill with green water.
Lusty frogs come back
to luscious grass.
Golden wolves join coyotes,
black bears make a pact,
to take back their territories.

Let flying marsupial fanged frogs
Grunting fish and wooly rats
Rush out of Bosavi crater in Papua.

Let earth go back
to its origins of
boiling mud ponds.

Let burnt demon souls
dance.

Wrong side

(after Alan Dugan)

I came out
on the wrong side of time
raping burning fields and forests
toppling arches red marble columns
into Caesarea port.

I came out
on the wrong side of the mirror.
A split face, gashed eye,
My ugly brother emerges
princess sister.

I came out
on the wrong side of the street,
dragged dead by a racing car.

I came out
on the wrong side of manhood,
a drummer dwarf
bleeding on the carpet.

I came out
on the wrong side of the woods,
cooked by a witch.

I came out
on the wrong side of Mexico City
(is there a right one?),
knifed by drug dealers,
finished off by police death squads.

I came out
on the wrong side of the equation,
minus brackets,
dizzied by graphs.

I come out
through shrinking, disappearing mountains
of Bibles, New Testaments. Qur'ans, Dharma.

I cut through languages, zipped through
old tablets warning of goddesses,
ran around deciphered cuneiform cylinders
stuck to royal hieroglyphs.

I came out
burning in a crematorium,
freezing to death in snow marches.

I came upon
a pagan of Yom Kippur,
God inscribed
in the Book of the Dead.

Brushes

(after Joni Mitchell)

I live in a paint box
squeezed between rusty cans.
Crayons pile up.
Brushes irritate my nostrils.

The box is flung open,
Olivia carelessly throws everything out,
looking for her balloon.

Flat on the floor,
run over by mice,
a hairy hand throws me back.
winds me.

A brush in hand
I paint the floor
from a split open pink can.
Crayons draw green purple circles.
The baby laughs and throws up.

At night, the garage is quiet.
The red Rambler, coughing oil,
dreams of another cross country,
marveling at the Grand Tetons
and the majestic Pacific shore.

Boots

(after Marge Piercy)

The dead move about the room as raindrops
turning into flurries collecting
dust specks in the corners.
Fixed on grandchildren,
photos on the walls.
Retreating
from the darkening window
to closets where they buckle their boots
for the mountainous journey.

When

When the kitchen floor is spotless
the refrigerator dishwasher humming
stains appear on the ceiling

The yard stays under twilight spell
trees stuck between seasons coated lightly with snow
leaves shiny brown under warm rain

The highway by the house shrinks to a donkey path
Weeds retreat underground with a whimper
Woodchucks move their families across the street

Not one squirrel to be seen
Cardinals, blue jays and finch pairs missing
Earthworms hang dry on a crumbling low stone wall

Synagogue mournful horn blends
with Romanian church requiem
cut by fire sirens

From the low hills
hyenas and jackals descend

About the Author

Hanoch Guy, Ph.D. Ed.D., spent his childhood and youth in Israel.

He is a bilingual poet in Hebrew and English. Hanoch is a Temple University emeritus professor of Jewish and Hebrew literature, and he has taught poetry and been a mentor at the Musehouse Center.

Hanoch Guy has published his poetry in the U.S., England, Wales, Greece, and Israel.

He has won awards from *Poetica, Mad Poets Society, Poetry Super highway,* and *Philadelphia Poets.*

Hanoch is the author of seven English poetry collections and a Hebrew poetry collection.

Other books by Hanoch Guy

The Road To Timbuktu: Travel poems. AuthorHouse, 2012.

Terra Treblinka. Holocaust Poems. AuthorHouse, 2012.

We pass each other on the stairs: 20 imaginary and real encounters. AuthorHouse, 2013.

Sirocco and Scorpions: Poems of Israel and Palestine. Aldrich Press, 2014.

A Hawk in Midflight. AuthorHouse, 2017.

Green Cow (in Hebrew). CreateSpace Independent Publishing Platform, 2018.

NOKADDISH in the Void. Ben Yehuda Press, 2019.

Website ~ www.hanochguy-kaner.com